Living Your Dream

A How-To Manual for Full Time RVing

by

Connie Gleason

ISBN #978-0-9837594-09

Front Cover Created by Janet Sieff
"Centering Corporation" in Omaha, NE

Library of Congress Control Number: 2012934291

LifeStory Publishing
P. O. Box 541527
Orlando, FL 32854

Printed in the United States of America

All grammatical and typographical errors have been put in this book for your enjoyment in finding them.

Have you ever said, when I retire, I am going to sell the house, buy an RV and travel? Well, we did just that. This book will give you some insight on how to start your own trek to begin your own travels on the road. What do you keep? What do you get rid of? And what do you do with it? All these questions and more will be addressed in this little book.

Making the change from homeowner to being on the road takes planning. Keep in mind we did all of this before eBay or Craig's List. We were making our plans in the mid 90's. It is actually a lot easier now with the computer and smart phones.

What fun you have in store for you as you begin to prepare for your new life on the road.

Table of Contents

Backing into an RV Lifestyle

We have been RVing for over 12 years now, almost half of that time, full time. So, how and why did we decide to do this lifestyle? We backed into it!

I worked for the airlines and we had wonderful travel benefits. We were either in the Orient or Europe every year. Times Square for New Year's Eve, a Las Vegas weekend for our 30th birthdays, a Ft. Lauderdale week-end in the middle of a snowy winter. And there was Bermuda. It was truly a wonderful life!

Then in the late 80's, I was transferred to a different reservation office. Little did I know that it was an allegedly sick building. By the mid 90's, I had permanent damage to my lungs (Restrictive Airways Disease or RAD) and was highly sensitive to colognes, perfumes, and other scents. (Multiple Chemical Sensitivity or MCS).

Grounded! I couldn't fly on a plane with scented people in an enclosed environment. I couldn't even breathe well enough to walk through the airport.

We tried Bed & Breakfasts on the beach. At the hotels and inns, We would ask if they had a "green" room, Plus, we also got tired of requesting "to smell" their rooms to see if I could breathe in them. It was just too difficult to travel, I was miserable.

That is when my husband, Ken, suggested a Recreational Vehicle. Whoa, I was not a camper. I was used to staying in resorts. Why would I want to camp?

With an RV I could control my environment, sleep on my own sheets without bleach and carry healthy food. It would work!

We started out by renting an RV for 3 days with the option of a month if I could breathe OK in it. Cruise America in Orlando was wonderful. They let me "smell" the RV's until I found one in which I could comfortably breathe.

We packed for the trip not knowing what we were doing, but having fun doing it. However, as we pulled out of our housing development, I was in tears. The sleek airliner had been replaced by a 23' lumbering camper. The road noises reminded me of the pots and pans flopping around on a Conestoga wagon like the ones I had seen in old western movies.

The first night I was so upset that I went to bed without dinner. This was a biggie for me as I am a foodie and never miss a meal. I was miserable as we drove past the Disney resort at Hilton Head where we normally stayed. Tears rose in my eyes as I realized that part of my life was over. Now, I was literally on a new road. I was beginning a journey of freedom and exploration in an RV.

Connie's Dedication

In 1995, Susie Pecuch was the first person to tell me that I was going to write a book. I poo pooed the idea. Yet, here I am with my first book.

Judy Rowley, my high school friend, asked me every time she saw me, "Is your book finished yet?" I thank them both for their faith in me.

It takes a village is definitely true about getting a book published. I have been to many writing classes and retreats, learning something new with each one. My writing "home" is Pat Charpentier's classes in Orlando.

Joy Johnson, my editor, who is my RV neighbor during the winter came into my life exactly as I was putting this book together. She gave me the inspiration that I needed to make this book actually happen.

Most of all to my husband Ken, my lover, and partner in life on this journey. He has been there every step of the way and was my technical adviser for this book as he formatted it for me.

On the Road Again

On the road again...
That old Willie Nelson song,
I sing it every time we start out again.

On the road again...
Destination unknown
Maybe miles to make,
Maybe just a few.

On the road again...
The coastline, the seashore,
Majestic mountains or the dessert sands.
Life on the road is so much more.
Unbelievable, living life to its fullest.

What to look for in a Recreational Vehicle

Buying an RV

What kind of RV do you want? Do you want a motorcoach or do you want to pull a unit? The decision was made for us as I needed to be able to lay down to rest while Ken drove, so we needed a motor coach. This eliminated the fifth wheel and trailers for us.

That just left us with what type coach did we want - Class A, B, or C? Since we were going to live in it, we had to have a larger unit, that eliminated the Class B or Road Trek/enlarged mini van or a unit that fit in the back of a pickup truck.

First we rented a motorcoach. It worked well. We came home and bought one just like it. We bought a 23' class C. The distinguishing factor here is the overhang (usually a bed) over the front windshield.

Next we upgraded to a 32' class A motor home. Big difference in the amount of space and driving the unit. We used this RV for summer travel until we decided to become full timers. Ken thought we should have a diesel motor to help in the mountains and we wanted a larger unit to live in.

Now, what kind of RV do you want - Fleetwood and all their models, Winnebago, Tiffin, Monaco, Holiday Rambler, Newmar, etc. It is like buying a car, there are Smart Cars and then there are Cadillacs. Top of the line is probably Prevost, but that was way over our budget.

11

Near us in Orlando is Lazydays RV Center. We stopped and looked and that is all it took as they have a well-oiled selling machine. They have a complementary dining area for their customers and potential buyers. Also a huge area for you to wait while you have your service work done. A Camping World is on property and they have their own campground. They have it all.

You start looking at floor plans. Do you want the living area in the front, what type layout do you want for the kitchen, where do you want the bathroom and how much closet space do you need? Do you want a washer/dryer, which way do you want the bed to face, what colors do you want? This is just the beginning of choices you will have on the inside.

Ken had definite ideas of what he wanted outside. The basement or storage space underneath comes with different type doors. Do you want them to open up or sideways? In some units the storage goes all the way through the coach in others it does not. Do you want the storage units to come out with your sliders? Ken did so he wouldn't have to crawl under the slider to get to the storage. Oh yeah, how many sliders or slide outs do you want? Do you want an outside TV, shower, and/or freezer? Decisions, decisions, decisions!

Even, after you have FINALLY selected an RV, when you get home you are asking each other, now, did it have that feature or not? You have seen so many floor plans that you can't remember. Once you get your unit, you will have fun exploring all the nooks and crannies, plus planning your future trips.

All you have to do is pick out your unit. Good luck!

Motorized RVs

Living quarters are accessible from the driver's area in one convenient unit.

MOTORHOMES

- **Type A Motorhomes**
  - Generally roomiest of all RVs
  - Luxurious amenities
  - Sleep up to six

- **Type B Motorhomes**
  - Commonly called van campers
  - Drive like the family van
  - Sleep up to four

- **Type C Motorhomes**
  - Similar amenities to Type As
  - Optional sleeping space over the cab
  - Sleep up to eight

SPORT UTILITY RVS
Available motorized and towable (as travel trailers or fifth-wheels).

- Built-in "garage" for hauling cycles, ATVs, and other sports equipment
- Sleep up to eight

Towable RVs

*Designed to be towed by family car, van or pickup truck. Can be
unhitched and left at the campsite while you explore in your auto.*

TRAVEL TRAILERS

- **Conventional Travel Trailers**
  - Wide range of floor plans
    and sizes
  - Affordable homelike amenities
  - Sleep up to 10

- **Fifth-Wheel Travel Trailers**
  - Spacious two-level floor
    plans
  - Towed with a pickup truck
  - Sleep up to six

- **Travel Trailers with
  Expandable Ends**
  - Ends pull out for roomy
    sleeping
  - Lightweight towing
  - Sleep up to eight

FOLDING CAMPING TRAILERS

- Fold for lightweight towing
- Fresh-air experience with
  RV comfort
- Sleep up to eight

TRUCK CAMPERS

- Mount on pickup bed or chassis
- Go wherever your truck can go
- Sleep up to six

Taking Possession of Your RV

The BIG day has arrived and you drive to the RV dealer to take possession of your new or slightly new RV. You are so excited!

After all the paperwork - did you just sign your life away? You get to play in your new coach. At larger RV dealers, they are set up for you to park your trade in, if you have one, next to your new unit. You will have 1-2 days to explore and get to know your coach, plus move in. A representative will come around and show you how to use all the gadgets and gizmos. Now, how did he say to use that, you will ask each other later?

The first time you drive that coach out of the parking lot, you are scared to death as it is BIG! You will get used to it, but go slowly at first. You are now an RV owner. Yahoo!

Another Opportunity-Renting an RV

This is exactly how we started out. Fortunately for us, that was before all the phone numbers and photos were painted on the RV. We had one small sign that said, Cruise America. We could travel incognito. They sure can't today in any of the rental units, but it is an excellent form of free advertising for the rental companies as we all notice them.

Comparison shop as you would for a typical vacation. We had been to an RV show where Cruise America had a booth. They answered our many questions and told us to stop by the office in Orlando. If we went on an off peak time, we could get a discount. That is what we did.

Ken's school got out earlier than most schools, so it was a lower time period. They helped us choose a size that would work for us and be in our budget. They worked wonderfully with my breathing problems to make sure they had a unit that I could breathe in.

16

They actually let me visit several units until I found one that worked for me.

Packing the rig is an experience as you have never done this before. But, it is like camping outdoors as you take a lot of the same things with you except you will have linens instead of a sleeping bag. You also have a bigger refrigerator than a camp size one.

There are three large companies that rent RV's which I have listed here. There are many smaller local companies also. Check online for the one that is near you. Here are the numbers and web sites for the largest 3 companies that rent RV's these days.

Cruise America
www.cruiseamerica.com   800-671-8042

Camping World
www.campingworld.com/rvrentals   877-297-3687

El Monte Rentals
www.elmonterv.come   888-337-2203

Camping World has become a big player in this arena. El Monte is more popular out west as they are located there, but I have seen their units on the east coast.

You know this worked well for us and we did exactly what the industry hopes everyone will do. We came home and bought an RV. This trip had given us the opportunity to be part of a different lifestyle that celebrates the pure joy of adventure and freedom. We loved being on the beach and visiting Civil War battlefields while in our "own" RV.

Happy Motoring if you try this method.

Lazydays RV Dealer

Our local RV Dealer is Lazydays near Tampa. We bought our current RV with them in December of 2004, when we started RVing full time. They have a huge operation there and have been a great help in the research for this book. The terms at the end of the book are what they give their new hires to become familiar with as they start their new jobs in the RV world.

Mr. David Castaneda, Training Manager, told us about Lazydays philosophy to help people experience their dream. They want people to feel at home here. They have a whole marketing campaign that makes you feel like you are coming home whether you are visiting as a potential buyer or for repair service. This organization has a big inventory of Class A, B, and C motorhomes, plus some towables. (See the RV Types Chapter for descriptions of each of these).

For the RVer's convenience they offer several on-site facilities such as a restaurant serving breakfast and lunch to clients and potential buyers, a Camping World Store, Thousand Trails Camping Club (membership required to stay at these campgrounds) and one whole end of the building is a lobby to wait in while your coach is being serviced. They have their own campground called, Lazdays RV Campground with a conference center. The newest addition to the campground is "Exit 10", a diner type restaurant in an

RV body. The bar is an RV awning with lights strung from it, of course. Just like RVers. You think you are inside your RV sitting in the slider having a meal, except you have a wait staff.

Lazydays offers seminars for their customers in their Learning Center. You can learn about water heaters, safe driving, etc. and future RV trips. We hope to be there next winter telling about our experiences with our new book in hand.

RV Driving

Insurance and Road Services

Just like car insurance, you must carry insurance on your recreational vehicle. But, a lot more money is at stake here. Plus, if you are full timing, where do you live while it is being fixed or replaced?

Go to a company that specializes in RV's. We had always used AAA for our road service and upgraded to include the RV when we purchased our unit. We kept that policy for several years until we used it.

We had been in Miami for the Super Bowl in 2007 when the Indianapolis Colts won. We had a fabulous week of fun and sun, plus celebrating a victory. On Monday, we revved up our engines and started to bring our slides in. The back bedroom slide would not budge.

After trying all the options we knew, we called AAA. We were in for a rude awakening as they wanted to tow it to a garage. Tow a 38' vehicle for a slider? Can't you picture that as it goes down the road with the slider out. We tried to explain to them that this was impossible, but they didn't get it as they were geared for cars.

Fortunately, Stout's RV in Indianapolis which is now a Camping World came to our rescue and told us how to manually get the slide in. On our next visit to Indianapolis, we got this problem fixed.

Make sure the company you are dealing with knows about RV's. Ask for recommendations from where you buy your RV, from Camping World, and from friends who have units. Check online also. The same goes for road services as you can see from our experience, it does make a difference.

Don't forget renters insurance. Yes, the RV insurance will hopefully pay for damages on the unit, but what about the contents? You are probably carrying at least one computer, a printer, TV's, jewelry, clothes, and all kinds of things that add up if you have to replace them. This is an essential that most people do not think about.

Driving

Don't feel comfortable driving your RV? Take some classes to learn how to drive a big rig. Search them out. We were fortunate that where we bought our unit, they offered driving classes. It was invaluable information for both of us.

Barney, at Lazydays taught us how to park, turn, and back up as each person in the class had the opportunity to experience these techniques. You may want to take these lessons even before you purchase your RV. Some of our friends took semi-truck driving lessons to be comfortable driving on the road.

Do whatever it takes for you to become familiar with your rig. Whatever you do, be prepared.

You cannot stop quickly.

Be alert at all times.

NEVER use the cell phone or eat while driving.

Now, I am a "straight" driver. That means, I only drive on straight roads. Ken does all the fuel stops, backing into parking slots, etc. I can relieve him if necessary. Besides what happens if Ken or your companion became ill and could not drive? This happened to some of our friends and she had to drive from Tennessee to New England without any experience. She had to learn fast when he got sick.

(You can buy insurance to cover this and a driver will get you home)

My husband is a fast driver in a car. But, as Barney says, where are you going in such a hurry? These rigs do NOT stop on a dime. You will also save on fuel going the speed limit. Besides the cars will pass you and they certainly will not slow you down. Always be aware of your surroundings as you drive too. You are sitting high and can see farther ahead.

When you are tired, stop. Usually, one of us is fresh as we change drivers frequently on the road. At one rest stop, we were both tired. You know what, we both napped. Within the hour, we were humming down the road again, much refreshed. What a life!

"Driving" to Ocracoke, North Carolina in the Outer Banks. The only way you can reach this island is by ferry.

Unusual Signs on the Road

Towed Vehicle (Toad)

We started out in a 23' Thor by Dutchman. As I mentioned, we rented one and liked RVing so much we came home and bought one similar to what we had rented.

Our first trip out, we rented a car at our destination. That is OK for awhile until you get used to driving the unit. But, you soon realize you want a smaller vehicle for in town traffic. You do not want to be in downtown Gatlinburg, Tenn in any size RV. Trust me on this one.

You start looking at small cars or pickup trucks to tow. Now, we had a Ford Ranger pickup and the color went with the RV. This is very important to RVers that their "toad" matches or is color co-ordinated to their unit. Ask any former Saturn dealer about this fact.

Saturns were built ready to tow with an easy hook up. Since Saturn is no longer in existence you start looking at other models. If you drive a straight stick, then this becomes easier. However, I prefer an automatic transmission and that requires more detail. We have a pump that circulates the transmission fluid while we tow and the car is out of gear. All of this can be done at Camping World, your new best friend. These days research can also be done online. Any RV magazine regularly runs articles on the best towed vehicle of the year.

Remember when you start to tow, you have just increased the length of your unit with a car or whatever you are towing. Each time you get longer, the maneuverability is less. In the 23', we could usually park on the street. Not so much in a Class A big rig towing a car. One time we stopped in a small Indiana town as we knew their German restaurant was good. We were the tourist attraction for the afternoon as everyone came out to see the "big RV" in town. In a Class B, you can pull into a drive up window at a fast food restaurant. We are too tall for anything like that.

Church parking lots are wonderful places to park and have lunch unless it is Sunday. They are usually big and empty during the week. We wanted to stop at Lincoln Memorial University in the Cumberland Gap. We drove through campus and didn't see anything suitable for parking. However, there was a lovely small church with a big parking lot across the street. We parked there, visited the Lincoln Museum and were happily traveling down the road in a couple hours.

You will see anything and everything towed. Some units are plain black or white, while others are color co-ordinated to the rig down to the pin striping. Some people pull a boat and/or gulf cart. I have included a few pictures here of some unusual towed items we have seen. You never know what you are going to see on the road.

Unusual Toads

GPS

I have been Ken's navigator for over 40 years now and vise versa. We are both good at reading a map and locating where we are and where we need to go. We have done this all over the world. Now, I have help, Gypsy, our GPS.

It is perfect timing now just when I can't see the maps as clearly. Gypsy tells us where to go, when to turn and what lane to get into. This is particularly helpful when you are in a big rig. Some newer big rigs come with them built in so that you do not have to purchase an additional unit.

We talked to a lot of other RVer's before we invested as they were just under $500 when we bought ours. The primary thing to look for is one that gives you alternate routes when you miss your turn. Some merely keep repeating missed your turn, missed your turn. You know that, now you need to know what to do next. Ours recalculates and gives us a new route. When you miss a turn in an RV you don't just make a quick U turn. These things don't turn on a dime as you know.

We bought a Garmin and have been very happy with it. This unit has the capability of directing a car or bus/RV with a flip of a switch. So, we keep it portable. It easily comes apart and we place it on an 8x8" bamboo cutting board. We placed rubberized shelving on the bottom of it to prevent it from sliding on the dash. We have a cute black cloth case with a handle on it which we bought at a box store in the make-up department. We take Gypsy on the road with us in the car and RV.

Garmin no longer makes this type of GPS. In order to have a larger vehicle denoted, you must buy a truck GPS. Then, you input the size of your bus, van, or truck. That way, it will not take you down any narrow roads.

Nowadays, you can own a GPS system for much less money as a single unit or even in your phone. That is on our short wish list for this year as they have improved significantly since we bought ours. They are now cheaper and smaller in size, plus come with their own case. This is an item where you want quality. Do not "cheap out" on this purchase or you could pay dearly on the road later.

We were at Tom Johnson's RV in Marion, North Carolina and our neighbor had the whole side of his RV scraped and the awning was ripped off. He had used a GPS that did not have bus or van controls. They had sent him down a narrow road and bridge. He had no place to turn around. You do NOT want to be in this situation. Plan ahead.

We want to try out our GPS in our iPad also. The screen sure is a lot bigger and they supposedly have stands or clips for them to adhere to your dashboard. I'll bet there is an app for that.

Repairs

It is not a matter of if you will need repairs, it is a matter of when you will need them. Where do you go for repairs on the road?

If you can schedule a stop at your RV's factory that would be ideal. Red Bay, Alabama for Tiffin, Forest City, Iowa for Winnebago, etc. But, what happens when you break down on the road?

Your campground office usually has a list of mobile RV services if your unit cannot be moved. The campground office or other campers will recommend someone local to drive the unit for service. Is there a Camping World nearby or an RV dealer? All of these work.

In Luray, Va., we had problems where we needed a mobile unit to come to us. The office helped us locate one. In SC, we had battery problems and we were on our way to a wedding in Savannah, Ga. There was a Camping World in Savannah. We made an appointment and had our work done before the wedding.

We had even more problems with the battery as we headed to New England. Sure enough, there was a Camping World there, they fixed the problem and it was covered under warranty since their company had just worked on it.

Plan your regular maintenance as you do your trips. We know there is a dealer in our hometown of Indianapolis, Stouts RV. It is now a Camping World and they are good to work with. We can see old friends while getting repair work done. We also use Tom Johnson in North Carolina as it is convenient for us. That is the good thing about having a towed vehicle. You can visit nearby places while they work on the RV.

If you are in a resort area and peak season, know that it is going to be difficult to get an appointment. Lazydays near Tampa is swamped in the winter when all the snow birds are in. North Carolina in the mountains in the summer is the same way. So, unless you have an emergency such as a water leak or something, you may have to wait awhile for repairs.

While looking for a repair place, today we can also use our computers or smart phones to find local repair shops. It is getting easier all the time.

Camping

Locating Campgrounds

Woodall's and Trailer Life are just a couple of places to research campgrounds. Both books are the size of an old Sears & Roebuck's catalog. They locate the campgrounds by city and state locations and rate them for you.

Today, you can do this online much easier if you have access to a computer, smart phone, or iPad while traveling. Check out the web site of the campground as some of them have virtual tours of their facilities or at the very least, pictures.

Word of mouth is a great way to learn about other people's favorite campgrounds. They will recommend where they have stayed and why they like it. Go online and participate in chats or RV park reviews. See where other people have stayed and why they liked the campground or why they did not.

Campgrounds

The Travel Channel's
Best Campgrounds in the United States

Durango RV Resort in Red Bluff, California

Boyd's Key West Campground in Key West, Florida

Horse Thief Lake Campground in Hill City, Black Hills,
    South Dakota

Rivers Edge RV Park in Fairbanks, Alaska

Yosemite Pines RV Park in Yosemite, California

Zion River Resort in Virgin, Utah

The Shady Dell RV Park in Bisbee, Arizona

Connie and Ken's Favorite Campground

Ft. Wilderness at Disney World in Orlando, Florida

Dry Camping

This is camping without being hooked up to water, electricity, or a sewer. This can be on a beach, out in the woods, or at a Walmart. Yes, you can overnight at Walmart and their sister company, Sam's Club in most areas.

There is 24 hour a day security and large parking lots to move the RV around. If you are using a Walmart, please be considerate. This is a courtesy they extend to us and some people abuse it.

I have seen RV's with their jacks down and their sliders out with lawn chairs sitting out front of the unit at Walmarts. This is not an RV park. It is a place of business that allows us to overnight there.

Make sure that you can park in their lot as some counties have laws against it. Osceola County in central Florida has such a law and it is the closest store to Disney World. One Walmart store in Pennsylvania would not allow RV's to park overnight as someone had dumped their black water tank in the parking lot. Not a smart move and cost the rest of us the privilege of using their lot.

We have used Walmart parking lots while on the road when we are arriving late and leaving early. We know the area and it is safe (always check that out). They are convenient and we can pick up groceries and other incidentals that we need.

A Walmart store is a great place to take a break during the day also. They are usually near an interstate interchange so you do not have to drive far. Again, big parking lots for easy in and out with a big rig. We can stretch our legs walking in the store to buy supplies and groceries. The newer Walmarts are even carrying Diesel fuel. Now, that is one stop shopping. There is even a book published showing where the Walmarts are located. It is <u>Walmart Locator</u> or you can check online. There is now an App for this.

We usually travel with a pretty full tank of water in case we dry camp somewhere. Always handy also if the campground is having problems with their water. This has happened to us twice at separate campgrounds and we had to rely on our internal water. Thank goodness we had an adequate supply.

The Corp of Engineers is also another inexpensive place to stop. We have not tried this yet, but plan to as we head west. Lots of other RVers have and highly recommend it. Again, there is a book for this <u>Camping with the Corp of Engineers.</u>

Another time you may dry camp is at an RV Rally or special event or at an RV show. If you are there for an extended stay, the event will sometimes have a "honey wagon" to drain your tanks. They come to your site so that you don't have to move your rig.

Checking In

Look for this sign for campgrounds on highways. This is the universal symbol that camping is at the next exit. Follow these signs off the highway to the campground. Larger campgrounds will have billboards and signs pointing the way also.

When we arrive at a new park, Ken unhooks our towed car while I check us in as I am the one who makes the reservations ahead of time. This comes natural for me after having been in the travel industry my whole adult life.

Some RV parks will take you to the lot and help you park, while others give you a map. Some even tell you to take the spot you want and let them know where you are parked. It depends on how full the park is during your stay and their policy. I like it when they lead you to the spot and help you park. That eliminates my job of assisting Ken into the parking spot.

Get walkie-talkies! Run, don't walk to the nearest store and buy a set. Don't stand behind the coach and yell directions to the driver. Always stand where the driver can see you and calmly talk into the walkie-talkie. We communicate by using "passenger side" and "driver side" as our directions rather than "left" and "right". These are just life savers. Cell phones could be used, but what happens if you are out of your long distance carrier's service area?

We only have one tip---Stop driving while you are still fresh. If you drive until you are exhausted, then you still have to set up. Not good. If something goes wrong, then the closest person to yell at is your partner.

Some days we may drive 300 miles, most days, we do not. What's the rush? Where are you going in such a hurry? I know, men like to get there. But, most RVers are retired. Enjoy the trip. So what if you only drive for a couple of hours. Do you really need to be somewhere that evening? If you do, plan your trip accordingly, otherwise, just enjoy the journey.

I always tell the campgrounds when making reservations that we are big and beautiful. It takes room to maneuver these units. Make sure that the campground can accommodate you.

Some campgrounds will say, "Oh, we can squeeze you in" Beware. At one state park in Indiana they told us this. My husband is very good at driving, parking, and managing this large unit, but he needs space. We finally got in the parking slot we had been assigned, but upon leaving, there was just no way he could get out. Fortunately, the sign post for the lot number was a 4x4. The neighbor and Ken rocked the post back and forth until they could pull it out of the ground. We drove out over the hole and then they put the post back. We all have road stories about our RV travels. Have you ever seen the movie, "RV" with Robin Williams? We can all relate to his comic efforts. If you haven't seen this movie, rent it now.

Back to setting up. When we arrive at our site, I am outside making sure the jacks go down. I watch as he lets the sliders out avoiding all the trees and wires. These are just good precautions. It is so much easier to spot potential problems than have your slider hit a tree branch or even the electrical post. Don't laugh, we have seen this happen. Again, all these things are easier to handle if you are not exhausted.

Ah, you have arrived. Ken is the outside man and I am the inside lady. He goes out to hook up the water, electricity, and the hose while I get things set up inside.

Trade duties every once in awhile to keep fresh on how to do all the jobs just in case you have to sometime. Can you hook up and unhook the sewer system, water, and electricity? Every adult traveling in the RV should know how to do these jobs just in case you need to use them.

Electricity & Things to Watch Out For

With the larger unit we use 50 amps. When we had the 23' Class C, we used 30 amps. Whatever you use, get a surge protector. These are not cheap, but they can protect your coach and its electrical contents.

One year we won tickets in the lottery to attend the Masters Golf Tournament in Augusta, Georgia. We booked reservations in the only nearby campground at that time. They were booked to the hilt trying to accommodate everyone for the tournament.

We had been assigned a parking slot out by the road and I was getting lots of diesel fumes. We asked them if we could move somewhere else and they accommodated us.

We had just moved when the electrical unit blew where we had been. It fried all the electrical appliances of the big rigs on that line without surge protectors. We learned real quickly that we must have a surge protector.

Last year when we checked into a Florida campground, our electrical unit was shot, but we did not know this. The first night, it blew and burned up our surge protector. All appliances were safe. That is why we carry a surge protector as there is not always consistency in campground electrical boxes.

Oh yes, the Master's was wonderful. It is mecca for golfers. Ken is a golfer and loved being there and I enjoyed seeing him so happy.

Water, Water Everywhere

There are three kinds of water in an RV. There is the fresh water that you carry to drink, shower and cook with when you are on the road and dry camping. There is gray water, that is what you have used in the shower, sinks, and the washer/dryer if you have one. Then, there is black water or sewage that comes from your toilet.

There is one hose that comes out from the basement of your unit. It splits as the gray water comes from one side and the black water is the other part of the Y. Ken always dumps the black water side first and then the gray water cleans out the hose as it flows through. You cannot dump either of these on the ground. You must hook-up to a sewer system. Now, you can have a full hook-up at most campgrounds with water, electricity, and sewer if you purchase that. Some only have water and electricity, there is a dump station on the way out of the campground that every camper can use.

 This is the universal symbol for a dumping station. In addition to your campground some filling stations offer dump stations. It is usually a Flying J, Loves, or Travel America (TA) that offers this service as they have specific areas for RVs. They sometimes offer propane gas also. A few states even offer dump stations at their rest areas.

Caution: The unit that holds the black water must be cleaned out regularly. Read your instruction manual on how to do this and you can get supplies at any RV store to do this procedure.

Here is Ken dumping at a central dump station at a campground in Virginia.

Drinking Water

Our coach has a water filtration system, plus we carry our own filter for me with Multiple Chemical Sensitivity. I cannot handle the chlorine that some campgrounds use in their water. You never know what type water you will get in some places, so be prepared to protect yourself. Most campgrounds are fine, but there is the occasional one that is not.

You can also put a filter on your kitchen sink faucet. Ours has a spray nozzle on it and I would prefer using it. Plus, the water filter also works in the bathroom, so I do not get chlorine in my shower water. That is important to me. It might not bother you.

Watch where you fill up your water tank. We once filled up with water under a wild onion patch. Our water smelled like green onions. We had to clean out our water tanks. You definitely do not want to do this often.

We carry bottles of water with us to drink. Now, if I am at a campground that we visit regularly and I have used their water before, then we use their water to drink. We both have aluminum refillable bottles to use to save the environment.

Before You Buy an RV, The Research

Simplify, Simplify, Simplify!

Get rid of clutter! This is for anyone, but especially true for potential full time RVers. You must downsize and get rid of some things. You just cannot drag a lot of stuff around with you. It saves on gas mileage and you just don't have room for it.

Give important things whether memories, collectables, or expensive things to your children. If you literally can't do that, loan them the china, silver, or furniture. Then, after you finish full timing, you have your prized possessions available to you. If you don't have children, like us, or if the children do not want the items, rent a storage unit. We had a unit for about 6 months until we could sell all our stuff.

Be ruthless as you sort. If it is in your hand, make a decision. Don't lay it down and decide later. It will not be any easier then.

Make a stack for garage sales. We sold lots of things at community garage sales. Make a pile to give away-Goodwill, Salvation Army, your church, your library, etc. Donate, donate, donate to all these charitable organizations. Remember to keep your receipts as they are all tax deductible if you file a long form. The last area is the circular file or the trash can. Use it frequently.

Some suggestions on what to do with certain items such as old high school yearbooks. We had some 1930's high school yearbooks of our parents. I wrote to the school to see if they wanted it. I always got an immediate reply that they would love to have the books.

What if the school is no longer in existence as is the case of Amboy High School? Then, look for a city or county museum. Miami County Museum in Indiana was happy to get yearbooks, graduation cards, and a diploma of a long ago school.

Parents that have saved clothes for generations- what do you do with all these things? We donated plaid polyester pants, wide ties, and checked jackets to a high school drama department. They were thrilled.

Aprons from my grandmother (bib style) and mother-in-law (jacket style), I couldn't give away. Today, aprons are popular again and we could have easily sold them.

Speaking of selling, use eBay, Craig's list, etc. In the early 1990's, these things were not popular or even in existence. Today you have the world at your selling fingertips.

Make friends with an antique dealer. This came about unexpectedly as I came out of exercise class. I stopped in to look around. Frank was an invaluable help to me sending me in the right direction to sell my goodies, everything from 78 records, old board games, jewelry, baby clothes, etc. Today, I could put these things online and not have to trek out with the items to each shop.

The 78 records did not sell, so I gave them to a guy in our housing development that liked music. I think he must have been a DJ when he was younger. Again, he was so happy to get them.

We had WWII uniforms. We tried the Women in Military Memorial in DC, but they did not need uniforms. Fortunately, we found a man in Orlando that does presentations for schools and uses the uniforms to show the children. He needed a ladies uniform, so we donated the outfit to him.

The whole idea is to get rid of stuff. However, you do it is up to you.

Kitchen

What kitchen utensils and appliances do you need in an RV? You don't want to carry as much as you would in a home as you just will not have the space to store everything.

Camping World, your new best friend, carries a set of stacking pans and a skillet. The handles are removable and interchange between the four different sizes of pans and the skillet. This saves a lot of space and I am glad that we bought them. We also kept one small skillet and another pan with a lip. That is it for cooking utensils.

We have a drawer of spatulas, grapefruit spoons, wooden spoons, etc. Watch what things you use on a regular basis and take them with you. Sell the others at garage sales or give them to family or friends.

We kept two cookie sheets that fit in our microwave/convection oven. Remember this does not have a huge cavity. It works great, but you cannot bake a full sized turkey in it.

Cake pans, one 9 x 9 for brownies, cakes, and the likes. two mini loaf pans and a muffin tin holding six muffins. Have you tried the new rubber like baking dishes? You can also bake in disposable aluminum dishes that you can buy at any grocery. We have two glass dishes to bake in and one glass mixing bowl that pours. These items are the extent of our glass things in the kitchen. Oh yes, we do have mugs, probably too many. We hung them from the ceiling inside of a cabinet so they will not break.

Tupperware, Rubbermaid, and anything unbreakable works great. Try to get some that use the same size lid, so you don't have to carry all different sizes. We have a hanger for the lids.

We do carry plastic wine and champagne glasses that we hang from a top cabinet. We have plastic, but I think you could hang glass without too much trouble. It depends on your lifestyle. If you use wine glasses a lot, you may want glass. Be as elegant or as plain as you want. This is your home now.

We bought a Cuisinart blender/food processor combination unit. It is one base unit with a food processor bowl and a blender top. That saves at least 1 big appliance space. We do carry a toaster and a griddle that converts to a panini maker and grill. We keep a crock pot in the basement (storage underneath the unit) to make soups when we have company and are gone for the day sightseeing with them. You come back home to a dinner fully prepared and it smells wonderful as you open the RV door.

Our refrigerator has an ice maker, so we do not need to carry ice cube trays. I buy things in plastic bottles from salad dressing to milk. If I can't find it in plastic, then I put them in a plastic one. I do this for soy sauce. Olive oil is the tough one as it is difficult to find in a plastic bottle (we have seen and bought it). It gets real oily and messy when you put it in a plastic pour bottle.

Spices, take the ones you need. You can always buy them on a trip and will find places where you want to buy fresh ones. We have ours in small plastic tubs in one cabinet. I have been looking at those tins that stick to a metal sheet and hangs on a wall. I haven't invested in those yet as I don't have a good place to hang it.

A lot of RVers grill outdoors. We simply do not for some reason. I wish we did, but we have never gotten into the habit. Some people use an electric skillet outdoors to keep the heat down in the coach while they cook. Some RVers even buy those 1 pot burners so they can cook outside. Some grills come with this type burner and it is all run on propane gas.

Basically, it is common sense. Take the utensils and appliances that you use. Neither of us drink coffee, so we do not carry a coffee maker. For coffee drinkers, this is an essential part of life.

After being on the road for awhile, go through your kitchen utensils and see what you are using. (This is actually a good idea for other things in your coach also) If something is not being used, get rid of it. If you need something, buy it if you want it.

We bought a knife holder that fits on the door at Camping World. One of the best things as it keeps our knives out of the spatula and spoon drawer. No one can get cut reaching into this drawer now.

Mail

What do you do with your mail while you are on the road? There are several different options for you.

Most people use their son or daughter's address. The children sort it and forward important information to you on the road at a destination stop. If this is not possible, there are mail services.

Escapees Travel Club offers this service to their members. You have a Livingston, Texas address which is their home office. They in turn forward the mail to you as requested. You can also get your license plates through the state of Texas. We refer to these people as "paper Texans". Family Motor Coach (FMC) offers this service also to their members. In each case of the above two companies you must join their group to use their mail service.

We opted to use a local mail service only because it was nearby. It works for us. We have a unit number there and they send out our mail whenever we call. They forward it to us wherever we are at that time. We are close to the mail center in the winter and we pick up our own mail.

We tried a US Post Office box, but that did not work as they cannot leave any package which requires a signature. The postal workers were great to work with, but it was not an advantageous address.

Just remember: wherever your address is, your auto insurance is based on the size of the city and/or the amount of traffic in the area. This could raise or lower your insurance rates.

The other thing an address provide is a place to vote. As a retired US History and Government teacher this is very important to Ken and me. It's a real privilege. Use it wherever you are.

Records and Not the Kind You Play

Where do you put your medical records? I have a loose leaf notebook where I keep x-rays of my left leg when I had a stress fracture and things like that. I want everything convenient for me so that I can pick up one folder and all the medical information is there. I am considering putting this information on a flash drive or somewhere in our iPhones. Haven't figured out quite the best system for this yet. Any ideas?

Passports and birth certificates are in a fireproof lock box well hidden in the RV. Oh yes, don't forget to carry your towed vehicle's title if you have one. One summer our towed truck gave out. We had to buy a car on the road and we had left the title at home as we had no intentions of buying a car when we left for the summer.

Our neighbor went into our home and got the document and mailed it to us. We now carry the title with us as we came home with a souvenir car that summer.

We also have a zippered black case similar to one that you would carry a passport in, above the front door in that storage area. I grab this black case and take it in with me when I check in to a campground. This is where we keep all our RV camping cards, our dog Molly's vaccination papers, and our registration and insurance card for the RV. I also put our license plate numbers in this case as the campgrounds usually want them and I can never remember those numbers.

What do you do in case of an emergency or storm? We have all important information scanned and we keep it in one CD case. It is easy to carry and we have the information in case we have to replace anything. You may want to make 2 of these CD's just in case one breaks or have a backup drive for your computer. Some people do both.

If you own your RV outright, then you would have the title to your RV also. Keep this in the fireproof lockbox also. Lucky you, that you own your RV. Most of us own them with the help of the mortgage companies.

Doctors and Dentists

We see doctors in Florida during the winter as that is where we are established. The doctor writes our prescriptions for a year's supply as he knows our lifestyle. His office staff knows that we are on the road (We take them edible souvenirs from our travel each fall) and they have been most helpful.

We arrive back in Florida usually the first part of November. We have an appointment with the dermatologist the Thursday before Thanksgiving. You may not need to do this every year, but we must as we have lived in the sunbelt for so many years. Plus, Ken was a swim coach and a life guard at Disney. He has had a bout with skin cancer on his leg. His Dad had problems with the tops of his ears from golf and Ken already has had to have some spots taken off his ears. A big broad band straw golf hat takes care of this problem. But make sure the big band has a lining or the sun will filter through the straw. We want to be pro-active and catch anything in the early stages. Ken also uses lots of sun tan lotion on his arms when he is outdoors for added protection.

The dentist, we see the Tuesday before Thanksgiving each year.   We always had our teeth cleaned every six months before. Now, we do it once a year as we are never in the same place in May for the six month check-up.

The optometrist we see over the winter months also. We both wear glasses and want to keep our eyes healthy.   We ask the doctor for a written prescription to take with us in case we need new glasses while on the road. At first, he was leery of this as people take the prescription and buy their glasses elsewhere. But, we explained to the doctor what we were doing and they were glad to help out. We keep the prescription in an old glasses case that holds the last pair of glasses that we wore. If you break your current glasses, you will go get the old pair and there is your new prescription.

Of course, as ladies, we need our check with the OB-GYN and mammogram. I do this each winter in Florida where my records are located. I am always glad to be finished with doctors and let out a shout as I visit the last one of the season. It is time to hit the road for the summer.

Medical Kit and Training

Why bother with a medical kit as you have everything with you? Some of them are cute and cleverly packaged, but usually expensive. Check to see what supplies they put in their kits. Do you carry all those supplies? If not, stock up to be prepared. Anything can happen on the road.

No ice pack and you have just sprained your ankle as I did? Use a bag of frozen peas or any vegetable to place on your ankle or wherever. You can also fill a zip lock bag with ice to create an ice pack. We also carry an All Temp Therapy Pack that we got from a chiropractor. They are wonderful and don't thaw out like the frozen vegetables. Plus, you can heat them in the microwave.

While you are in research mode for your RV, start taking Cardiopulmonary Resuscitation (CPR) and first aid classes. These are both good things to know on the road and in everyday life. Travel with competence and confidence that you are well trained in this area.

When you take CPR classes, they also teach you how to use Automated External Defibrillator (AED). I can see RV's coming with these in the future. Right now they are very expensive, but check them out and see if you think it would be a good investment. Also, check with your doctor as he/she may prescribe one.

Medicine and Illness

By the time we reach this age, we are all usually on some kind of medications. How do you get your meds on the road? We use a nationwide pharmacy.

In Florida and in North Carolina we have a CVS nearby. We chose them for location. Walgreens and Wal-Mart do the same thing. (Have you seen those long lines at the pharmacy at Wal-Mart? This was a detouring factor for us.)

My insurance company wants me to use their pharmacy and mail me the meds and it may be cheaper. However, that doesn't work as we don't know where we will be. It matters if we don't get our medicine on time. Mail can wait, medicine can't.

Some RVers travel frequently out of the United States to get their medicines at a cheaper price. We have not checked into this as we are fortunately not on many regular prescriptions. Is it a possibility? Check into it and see if it works for you.

What happens if you become ill on the road? If it is an emergency, call 911 immediately. If not, check with the campground office to recommend a nearby doctor or hospital. Pull out that trusty GPS system that you invested in or use your cell phone to find the nearest hospital if the office is closed. Other campers are resources as some of them may know the area.

Your RV family, the campground, will rally around you in cases of emergency and illness. We all know what it is like to be on the road and ill. Not fun, and friends are a great help in these times.

Connected

When we sold our home in 2004, we went to a totally cell phone system. We had no choice as there was no place for a land line. This system has worked well for us.

Cell Phones

We have a contract with ATT for our cell phones and a data card for the computer. You do not need a data card, but it makes life so much easier. We can be online anywhere ATT has service. Ken can be driving down the road and I am looking up campgrounds or keeping up with friends on Facebook. Most cell phone carriers have similar systems. Purchase the one that works for you.

If you do not have a data card with a phone company, then you have to rely on libraries, restaurants, coffee shops, or whatever store offers free wi-fi. A lot of campgrounds now offer wi-fi either free or for a slight fee. If you are not a full-timer, you may just want to use these services.

Computers

We had always been PC users, but our friends had these great Apple computers and we splurged and bought a MAC computer about 4 years ago. It was the best thing we ever did. Not cheap, but the services are wonderful.

For Christmas that year Ken bought me the $99 package of a year's classes on my new Apple computer. The training is fantastic! Who knew that I would ever have a web site and a blog. Certainly, not me who didn't grow up with computers. This is a whole language for baby boomers to learn. Now, I sit here and compose my book totally on my laptop.

Smart Phones

iPhones, another splurge, have become part of our lives. With the access to the internet, we can get our email anywhere. We first bought a portable phone for safety purposes when I was driving on the interstate to work for the airlines. Now, the first thing in the morning, I check the news with CNN or any other major news network. Ken even has news alerts coming to his iPhone. You can stay connected to the world if you want.

E-readers

Our latest purchase has been an iPad. Ken wanted one and I wanted an e-reader. Well, it is the ultimate e-reader. I chose it as I can download books from any of the services and the library. Plus, it is a bigger page than most of the e-readers. I bought an anti-glare covering and have no problems with it. Also, as I mentioned in the GPS pages, we want to try that with the larger screen.

When you buy a Nook, Kindle, Sony, iPad, or any of the popular e-readers, check to make sure that you can download books from your local library. At this time, most of the e-readers do, but not all.

Photographs

How many of you have albums of pictures or just lots of old photographs waiting to be put in albums? We all do. Thank goodness for the digital age where we can store them on the computer. They are probably still not sorted, but at least they are not physically sitting in a room in our home.

For birthdays we have been receiving cards with photos from our friends. They have been sorting out and getting rid of their old photos. Send them to your friends with notes about what good times you had together at the events in these photos. They make you smile and remember the good times together. Plus, they have gotten rid of their old pictures, you now have them.

We have another friend that uses the old photos for her Christmas cards. It is such a treat to receive her card each year to watch her and her husband grow up. She started with baby pictures and now is into elementary school years.

Scrap-booking is so popular these days. Collect photos of each child, grandchild, friend, or however you want to sort them. Make a scrapbook to give to each person at holiday time. The memories of each person will come flooding back as you make them their special book.

We have some really old photos from the early 1900's and even a couple of tin types that we just do not want to get rid of. Store these few photos with a friend or child while you are on the road. Save them as they are priceless.

Do you know who all these people are in these old pictures that you are saving? We were fortunate as Ken's Mom wrote names and relationships on all the old pictures that she had and that we have inherited. Sorry to say, we do have pictures from my side of the family that are not labeled.

Scan photographs into your computer and store them on a disc. I did this for each of our childhoods. Ken and I want to keep these cherished memories, yet we do not want to stumble over them in the RV.

These are just some suggestions with what to do with all those photographs that we have collected over a lifetime. While you are still working and doing your research on which RV you want to buy, you can be accomplishing this task.

Note: Discs only last so long and they do break. Either make 2 discs or recopy them in about 5 years.

Clothes

What clothes do you keep and what do you get rid of for RV travel? This lifestyle is very casual. We dress in layers as the weather gets colder or take off layers as it gets warmer. Keep in mind as I talk about what we keep, we usually are not in winter weather. We think snow is a four letter word and do not want to see our RV in it. If your lifestyle includes more cold weather, you would need to adjust what clothes you keep.

Coats:
1 winter
1 jeans Jacket
2 water proof jackets (1 heavy and 1 lighter)

All except the jeans jackets have hoods. That way if I get in a cool windy place, I just pull up the hood. I keep the lighter water proof jacket in the car. You end up storing a lot in your towed vehicle.

Slacks:
2 pairs of jeans
3 pairs of zip off pants.

I love zip off pants. I can start out in a pair of slacks with a sweater combination on cooler mornings. By mid afternoon when the weather gets nice, I am in shorts and a tank top as my "legs" and cardigan have come off.

Capri Pants:
3 pairs - Navy and 2 bright colored ones

Shorts:

Ken says I own way too many pairs of shorts. As a Floridian, you have different length of shorts depending on the weather. So, I have longer shorts, dress shorts, and knit driving shorts. For the latter, you want something comfortable as you will be sitting in the RV for hours as you drive down the road.

We try to do laundry about once a week. I carry enough underwear and socks for 10 days. I try to buy white underwear so that I can wash it with the white socks and do them all in one load. I carry extra just in case we are not near a laundry or electricity for our machine.

Sweaters:
    2 long sleeve sweaters for cold weather
    1 sweatshirt

Dress clothes:
    1 good black dress for funerals and/or
        weddings
    1 pair dress black slacks
    1 dress jacket
    1 tailored white blouse
    2-3 sweater sets in bright colors to wear
        with slacks or jeans

We do lots of things at Purdue University, so I have black and gold dress clothes. I don't wear them often and we have found the vacuum bags work wonderfully. Simply suck out the excess air with your vacuum cleaner tube and layer the bags in the basement of the RV. The clothes are ready when you want to take a cruise or need special event clothes.

Ken and I do lots of volunteer work. You need a pair of khaki slacks (I use zip offs) and a pair of black slacks as most places require either one of those colors and they usually provide a t-shirt or golf shirt.

Dresses:
1 black sundress
1 flowered sundress with shrug

I usually buy 1 outfit that is popular for the season. This year flowered dresses are in style. Since I am going to a wedding and a party, I bought a new dress with a shrug.

Shoes:
1 basic pair of tennis shoes

We buy new tennis shoes each winter as we wear them a lot. I take the old pair and put them in the trunk of the car with socks. That way I have a back up pair of shoes and always have tennis shoes with me as we drive.

1 pair black dress shoes
1 pair dressy brown sandals
    different colors of sandals for everyday
1 pair of hiking boots
1 pair of knitted slippers with grippers on
    the feet

These are helpful as you travel to keep your feet warm and not slide as the RV moves.

Clothes for Ken:

Coats:
        1 winter coat
        1 jeans jacket
        2 water proof jackets (1 heavy and 1
                lighter) with hoods

Slacks:
        Gray dress slacks
        Black slacks
        3 pairs of zip off slacks for golf
                1 is khaki for volunteering.
    Jeans:

Ken has several pairs as he wears them
frequently. He has everyday, dress, and work jeans.

    Shorts:

Ken complains that I have too many, but he
has quite a few pairs also. Although, he wears jeans
more than shorts.

    Shirts:
        Golf shirts

Ken has several of these shirts as he plays golf
in these when you need a collared shirt. He also
accrues the different colors when he volunteers at the
Arnold Palmer Invitational and Disney's Children
Miracle Network Classic golf tournaments.

        1 dress white shirt
        2 dress shirts both go with a black suit
        T-shirts (Many as this is his standard
                wardrobe with a pair of jeans.)

3 flannel shirts

He layers these with t-shirts when it is cold.

Sweaters:
        2 sweaters (1 red for holiday wear)
        1 sweatshirt

Suits:
        1 dress black suit

Shoes:
        1 pair tennis shoes
        1 pair black dress shoes
        1 pair brown loafers
        1 pair hiking boots
        1 pair crocks that he wears to walk Molly

24/7

For Better or Worse, For Richer For Poor, but the preacher did not say anything about being with your spouse 24 hours a day, 7 days a week in a confined area. That is what happens when you live in an RV.

You must be compatible before you hit the road. If you argue at home, you will argue on the road. Actually, there is probably more to fight about as you are in a smaller space than a normal sized house. Plus, you are together more hours in the day.

My father-in-law retired from the government many years before my mother-in-law. He always said, he was retired until she retired and then he was just plain tired. She planned lots of activities for him and he was used to his own schedule. It took an adjustment period for them and it will for you also.

Ken and I had been used to sharing close quarters together during the summers as he was a school teacher. We had been RVing since 1998, so we had some idea of what we were getting into. Plus, we have no children, so we were used to spending lots of time together. We were married in 1967, so we have been fortunate enough to spend lots of summers together and since 2004 on the road full time.

Still, there are times when you need a break from each other. Ken loves to watch TV and sports in particular. I would rather be outdoors, so I am, if the weather is nice. I take a book (now my new e-reader) or project outside. Molly and I walk visiting the neighbors in the campground. I am much more social than my husband and this works out perfect for us.

As Oprah says, we need our girlfriends and time with them. While in Florida, I visit with old friends that I knew when I lived there full time. We usually have lunch out, plus try to take a walk and/or get in some type exercise. While in the mountains of North Carolina, I visit with friends that we used to know in Florida that have moved there.

I take cooking classes, craft classes, and do volunteer work if I am in an area long enough. I enjoy people and like to be around creative people.

Ken's outings are usually geared around golf. He gets to play some of the best courses on off days as a retiree. He meets new people while enjoying his golf game. In Florida, he golfs in the winter with a teaching buddy with whom he stays in contact. Another teaching friend and Ken have lunch together about once a month. It is very important to nourish friendships on the road. The computer with email, Facebook, twitter, and texting is an excellent way to stay in contact with friends also.

Whatever you do, plan some alone time for each of you. Sometimes I just need quiet time and so does Ken. That is ok. Go to one end of the RV or outside and do whatever you want. Right now, Ken is reading on the couch as I am typing at the desk. This works for us. We are comfortable in our cozy RV for the evening.

But, when you need time apart, take it. You will both come back more relaxed and ready to share your adventures with each other.

Miscellaneous

Giving Back

Just because you are on the road doesn't let you off the hook to give back to society. How you do that is up to you. We like to volunteer in areas that we visit particularly if we are there for a month or so.

We are frequently in Black Mt., North Carolina near Asheville. We volunteer at the Black Mt. Arts Center, Montreat, and at Warren Wilson College.

The Swannanoa Gathering Music Weeks is held for 6 weeks at Warren Wilson College. Ken has learned to play the mountain dulcimer and we both enjoy the music festival. Many evenings I will be typing on this book as he plays the dulcimer in the background for us. Just sweet.

In Florida during the winter, we volunteer through the Retired and Senior Volunteer Program (RSVP). We usher at events, plays, ballets, and operas. We do our jobs and then we can stay for the program as a benefit. We love doing this.

We also host Elderhostels, now Roads Scholars. I got involved with Elderhostels when I was an undergraduate at Indiana University in my 30's. One of my internships was involved with this program and I loved working with the seniors. They had successfully maneuvered through life and were having a ball in their senior years. They were role models for me.

We have gotten involved with Elderhostels in North Carolina and Florida hosting in each place. This is perfect for us as I was a tour escort when we first moved to Florida and Ken has chaperoned many eighth graders to Washington DC for their first trip to our Capitol. We love doing this and meeting all the interesting people.

Whatever you want to do to give back is what you should do. Some people help build houses with Habitat for Humanity, others work through their churches for missionary work. A lot of denominations have youth retreat centers with campgrounds. You can park there for free while you help open up the area in the spring and/or close it up in the fall after the summer session.

These are just a few examples of volunteering. There are just all kinds of possibilities. President Bill Clinton says that the baby-boomer generation has been known as the "me" generation. He thinks that our ultimate title will be the generation that gives back. We have been able to retire younger (hopefully) and have more free time now. We can give back. Let's do it!

Hair

Where do you get your hair cut while on the road? I always ask for a recommendation at the campground office. A lot of times, local beauticians will have their business cards in the office for you.

If all else fails, we go to a walk-in beauty shop. We have had some great haircuts in these places and then some not so great. One of the best haircuts was at a Wal-Mart walk in shop in southern Maine on I-95. We were overnighting there on our way home and walked into grocery shop and saw the beauty shop. There was no waiting line, so both Ken and I got our haircut.

Always remember, hair grows out quickly. So, if you get a bad haircut it will only last a few weeks. It's cosmetic surgery that heals itself.

Laundry

This is not your typical laundry at a campground. Look at all those machines. However, we did come across this facility in Los Angeles. Most RV parks have 2 or more washers and/or dryers. We have even come across outdoor laundries in the south. The machines are outside with just a roof overhead. It must be a warm climate for this type of set up.

Check the laundry area out before you drag your clothes down there. Is it clean and is it available? Always check the tub before you load up the washer.

Stay with your laundry. Take a book, chat with the other RVers doing their laundry or catch up on your email, play games or whatever on your smart phone.

We are always courteous and expect others to be and they usually are. But, every once in a while you run into someone rude or on a time schedule. Just accept them for what they are and realize they are in a hurry. Aren't you glad you don't have to be anywhere?

While folding your clothes and waiting for the spin cycle to stop, you can learn valuable information about the local area. Where have other RVers eaten out and would they recommend the restaurant. Look around for flyers of local points of interests, pet grooming, beauty shops, etc. A lot of parks have their book area here. Drop off a book and pick up a book.

No one wants to be carrying around books after we have read them. I leave current titles in laundry rooms and have found great books there also. Some people even leave DVD's.

Quarters become gold. Most laundries have a change machine for dollar bills. But, they don't always work. Be sure to carry your quarters with you. We use a dispenser for Necco Wafers (hollow tube just the right size for a stack of quarters).

Most RVers have a collapsable roller basket with them. Put the detergents, spotters, and softeners in the basket and stack your laundry bag on top. Roll it to the laundry room-very helpful in the mountains. A lot of campers use net bags with heavy duty handles so the clothes have air circulating around them.

We usually do laundry about once a week wherever we are. If you are dry camping every city has laundromats, especially college towns. There you will have plenty of washers and dryers so you can do many loads as you want.

We have a stackable washer/dryer in our RV. It is great for emergencies, but not big enough for a full load. It is great for drying towels after a day at the beach or in rainy weather when everything is damp.

Some laundry rooms close at night while others are open 24/7. We can do a small load in our washer and dryer after hours if we need something.

The new large RV's (usually over 40 feet) may have a residential size washer and dryer. These rigs have a tag axle in the back to accommodate the weight of the machines.

Laundry is laundry - a chore at home or on the road. Do it when you have plenty of time. Sit on the porch swing outside the building and enjoy your new location while your clean your clothes.

Vet's and Pets

Like most RVers we travel with a pet. Ours is a 10 lb. ball of white fluff named Molly. She is a Bichon Frise. This is the first dog that we have that we did not get from an animal shelter.

The pulmonary doctor recommended Bichons, Poodles, or Chihuahuas as I was having problems breathing around dogs after my illness. We knew nothing about the Bichon breed, but fell in love with them immediately.

Their temperament is wonderful for families and they are such sweet dogs, plus they are so cute. We had a rescued dog before that looked like a black Benji that weighed under 20 lbs. We wanted a smaller dog this time and Molly is perfect for us. She is a smaller Bichon as they normal weigh about 15 lbs. Although, we have seen Mickey, who is a Bichon at 25 lbs. So, they do vary. Plus, it depends on how much you feed them.

Speaking of that, let me get on my soap box here. Don't overfeed your dog! They are uncomfortable and it shortens their lives. Some poor little doggies can barely walk they are so rotund. Their masters have given them too much food. I joke that I do much better keeping Molly thin and trim than I do with my diet. If your dog is overweight, you probably are not getting enough exercise either.

Bichons are lap dogs. Supposedly, they came from France and were the king's dogs. Well, they are loyal and love to sit with you. On the days when I do not feel well, Molly knows and lays right along side me on the couch. She also gets me out walking as she needs exercise. It is a good excuse for both of us to get outdoors.

This type of dog works for us. I have seen people travel with cats, birds, and much bigger dogs. Joy and Marv, our neighbors and my editor has a Swiss Mountain Dog in their Fifth Wheel. Barney is 120 pounds and that works for them. Some people even have multiple large dogs in their coach.

How they have multiple pets is beyond me as there is not a whole lot of space in an RV. We keep Molly's bed under the bench table and it is her safe place out of the way. However, she sleeps anywhere in the RV that she wants. When we come home, she is sitting in the passenger seat looking for us. What a greeter.

No matter what kind of pet you have, think about their needs on the road. Carry their regular food with you. Their environment has changed, keep everything else familiar. The animals are usually fine as long as their owners are around, but it is best to keep a routine for them.

We use rubber bottomed bowls so they will not slide while we are traveling. In the car, we keep collapsable water-proof bowls for her as she travels with us on day trips. Molly knows the words "road trip" and how all 3 of us head for the car and a day of adventure.

We carry combs and brushes for her as Bichons are high maintenance. We have a dog groomer that we use about once a month in Florida, but otherwise we are on the road when she needs grooming. Ask at the campground office to recommend a groomer as they usually have pets and/or know of a local groomer.

Research this as it is important. I visit a groomer before I leave Molly. Always make sure they do not use automatic dryers as sorry to say this happened in Orlando at a nearby groomer. Pet people look away as this is sad. The automatic dryer did not go off and they literally "baked" the dog. You never think about losing a pet when you drop them off at a groomer.

I had checked out this particular groomer and I had decided not to leave Molly there. Boy, am I glad. This is an isolated incident as most groomers are pet people and will do anything to make your pets visit more enjoyable.

We started traveling from Orlando as that is the last place we had jobs, so Molly's vet is there. Dr. Doug Jones has been our vet since the early 90's. He is a fellow alumni from Purdue University and we are very happy with him. Before we hit the road each spring we visit Dr. Jones and get Molly's shots for the year. That way we start out with current records.

Always keep a copy showing proof of the shots that your pet has received. We have the current rabies tag on her collar along with a tag with our phone number on it in case for some reason she gets loose. You must have a health certificate issued recently to get into Canada. Check the rules before you go. Always tell the vet where you plan to visit as some areas are prone to different diseases. One year Molly had to have a Lyme Disease shot.

After Hurricane Katrina and the loss of so many pets, microchips became a very common way to track dogs. Those with chips were the major reason they were returned to their owners. Sorry to say, those without chips did not fare so well.

We have had our share of visits to animal clinics also. Make sure the vet you visit on the road is a member of American Animal Hospital Association (AAHA). This is similar to visiting a Board Certified Doctor. You know they are well trained.

Molly had to have surgery last fall as she had a growth between her pads on her left paw. We lucked out as one of our friends had moved from Orlando to Piney Flats, TN plus she worked at Appalachian Animal Hospital.

They were so helpful to us and got her fixed up just fine, but we are so glad that we didn't wait until we returned to Florida for the winter as we thought about doing and working with Dr. Jones. The growth was malignant and a fast growing kind. They got it all and she is fine now. Thank goodness.

The basic rule is take care of your pet. That includes picking up after your dog. Some beaches and campgrounds are not allowing pets anymore because of a few inconsiderate people. This is your pet and your responsibility.

Love your pet, keep a normal routine for eating, and exercise them. They will travel many miles with you and be a joy for your family.

This is the most unusual pet we have seen while on the road. This is Princess Confetti, a miniature horse, that is a service animal for it's owner.

What do you call your RV?

Do you name your car? Most people do name their RV's. We call ours Sagebrush as it rolls along stopping at different spots for awhile and then continuing on down the road. It is also green and I equate that with plant life.

Our "toad" is a silver PT Cruiser that Ken calls, Bullet. We have a western theme going here which is so funny as we have not lived in the west.

My ringtone for Ken is "The William Tell Overture" or the Lone Ranger theme song. He loves this song for both reasons as he likes the music and used to watch the Lone Ranger TV show as a child. I think of Prince Charming on a white horse when he calls. Plus, my regular ringtone is "The Good, the Bad, and the Ugly". A true western theme.

RV Museum

Take exit 96 at Elkhart off the Indiana toll road for this museum. This is an easy off and on stop as the building is located right at the I-80/90 exit. The exhibition hall is all about RVing, the pleasures, the present, the past, and the future.

The first display talks about current RVing with new models available for you to walk through. They show how to explore life on the road in an RV in this hall. There is a Supplier's Hall at the end of the building with products used frequently by RVers. The RV Founders Hall sponsored by Winnebago/Thor is a homage to the history of RVing.

They have 1913 trailers for Model T's, a 1929 Covered Wagon Travel Trailer, and other examples throughout the decades. Some you will recognize such as the 1950's Airstreams and the 1954 Holiday Rambler motorcoach. There are samples of all types of travel trailers, pickup truck toppers, and motorcoaches.

After the World's Fair in Chicago in the 1930's, Elkhart became a place where travel trailers were built. This industry and it's suppliers continued to grow in this area and is a prominent force in Elkhart and the surrounding areas economy even today. Here is a list of RV Manufacturing tours as of 2011 near Elkhart, Indiana.

Carriage	www.Carriageinc.com
Damon	www.DamonRV.com
Dutchman Corporation	www.Dutchman-RV.com
Forest River	www.ForestRiverinc.com
Thor Motor Coach	www.Thormotorcoach.com
Gulf Stream	www.GulfStreamCoach.com
Hy-Line Enterprises	www.HylineTrailers.com
Jayco	www.Jayco.com
Keystone	www.KeystoneRV.com
Heartland RV	www.heartlandrvs.com
Monaco Coach	www.Monaco-Online.com
Newmar RV	www.NewmarCorp.com
Renegade RV	www.Kibbil.com
Sunnybrook RV	www.SunnybrookRV.com

In addition to the tours, you can pick up anything you need from the nearby suppliers. One neighbor at the RV park was there for a new couch, one for some repairs, and many were attending an RV rally. This is the perfect place for a rally with a tour of their unit's factory.

You are also close to the Indiana Amish area. Definitely worth a stop in Nappanee, Middlebury, or Shipshewana. The home cooked food is fabulous, (no dieting here) and there is a general auction on Wednesday in Shipshewna.

Serious Stuff

Safety

Have you ever heard of their RV being broken into, neither had we; but it happened to us.

I was home alone at the Indiana State Fairgrounds. We were from Indianapolis and know the area. We kept our basement doors locked and our bikes securely locked up.

I came home from the grocery store at dusk as I did not want to be out at night in this area. I saw something on our front steps as I pulled up. I first thought it was from the cottonwood tree, however, it was the broken glass from our front door. I screamed and Molly, our dog, barked. I was so happy to hear her. She had gone under the table when the intruders came in. We lost a laptop computer and jewelry during the robbery.

It was a quick job as they could have taken more. The insurance representative said they wanted something they could sell quickly for drug money.

Since Ken was at Gettysburg for a Civil War Re-enactment, I had to drive the RV to a dealer to get a new window for the front door. I am sure glad that I knew how to drive the rig. Stout's RV, now Camping World, in Indianapolis took good care of me as I was scared and alone. I was really glad to see Ken when he got back into town.

The one thing we learned from this experience is to pull up your steps when parked in a public place. If our steps had been withdrawn, the robber could not have reached inside to use the handle to open the door even if they could break the glass. We faithfully retrieve our steps now.

Storms

The best advice for being in bad weather is, don't be in it. But, occasionally, you are out on the road and drive into a storm. On the whole though as retirees, we just wait until it stops raining. It is not much fun unhooking or hooking up your rig, plus attaching your towed vehicle while dodging rain drops. Grab a good book and a blanket, curl up on the couch and enjoy the time. Fix some comfort food like a grilled cheese sandwich and tomato soup while putting on some of your favorite music. Ah, life is good!

We had tornadoes while living in Indiana and hurricanes while living in Florida. Neither are fun, but at least you know when a hurricane is coming. They say, you are not a true Floridian until you have been through a hurricane. We have been through five.

Erin came through in the mid 90's and we went to the shelter at Ken's high school. Now, Ken had keys to his room as he was still teaching, so we registered, but slept in there in our sleeping bag. We even took Molly, our dog.

Hurricanes actually helped us make our decision to become full time RVers. Ken went back to school in August of 2004 as excited as ever for the new school year to begin. By November, he had decided this was his last year of teaching. We had 4 major hurricanes in 6 weeks.

Charlie came first, breezing in shortly after school started in August. His school, Poinciana High School, lost the roof of their gym and cafeteria. All the sporting events had to become "away" games., plus each team had to find places for their practice. Not even the football field was usable as the field's lights were dangling everywhere. All their lunches were taken in a huge "circus" tent set up for them. Thank goodness we were in Florida and the weather was warm enough to do this.

Personally, we lost lots of trees, electricity, and water. Ken couldn't even get out of our driveway as there were big trees down on it. We were fortunate that none came down on the house. I was in North Carolina and we could not talk for days until phone service was restored. Not fun to be separated from your loved ones in a state of emergency. The TV stations report where the storm is plus they keep you hyped up with sensationalism about the potential incoming weather. You, or at least I, cannot keep watching it as it keeps you in constant turmoil.

Next came Frances, Ken flew out on one of the last flights out of Orlando before they closed the airport. He came to pick me up in North Carolina. This was Labor Day week-end 2004. We left NC in rain as Frances headed for them and caused lots of flooding there.

Ivan was next and Ken didn't want to ride out another storm at home. We left in the RV heading north. Evacuating is NO fun! You are in lines of cars driving away from the storm. Emergency lights flashing about getting fuel, so as not to run out, plus what areas even had fuel. It was a zoo.

We had only been on the road a day, a very long day, when Ivan headed for the panhandle. We returned home. Glad to be back safe and sound.

Jean was the last hurricane of the season. We decided to stay home after the Ivan fiasco. We pulled the RV up near the house, fortunately not the side that the wind came from.

Whack, thump, what was that? The eave clapping against the house, we think. R-i-i-i-p, the roofing tiles slamming through the screened in porch. It all sounds eerie in the dark as we were holed up in our walk in a closet. Oh, we never want to do this again.

Enough, says Ken after the fourth hurricane passed. If I weren't teaching, we wouldn't be here. How true. We put the house on the market and it sold within a week just as the housing market was exploding in Florida. It was time for us to leave.

We were to be out of our house by New Year's Eve. We handed the new owners the keys to the house and started out on our new life on the road on Dec. 31, 2004. Ken taught the second semester as we became familiar with the coach. We hit the road once the school year was out and we never looked back.

Where did we spend the next hurricane season as Wilma went through Florida? In Atlanta, far, far away from the hurricane winds, traffic, and crowds.

When you check into a campground, the last thing you are thinking about is extreme weather. Ask if they have a shelter area to go to in the event of a bad weather. Most campgrounds do have a large room in a stationary building where campers could gather. Can you bring your pet in a kennel? Most campgrounds will not allow pets in a building.

Does the campground have a warning signal to let you know about upcoming storms? I have never stayed in a campground with such an alarm system. Does your smart phone have a radar system, some do. If all else falls and the weather stations are predicting bad weather, go to a hotel that will take you and your pet. We did this recently as a strong storm was coming through our city.

We also carry a weather radio in the RV to alert us of possible bad weather in our area.

Lemon Law

What happens if you truly have a "lemon" RV that you purchased? It depends on the state in which you bought it. Some states actually have no lemon law, others do.

We had a leak on the right side of the windshield from day one with our current RV. They worked and worked on this problem and it continued to leak every time it rained. We got the manufacturer, Fleetwood, involved also and were considering filing under the lemon law protection in our state of Florida when the problem was finally resolved. We were relieved as this is a very lengthy and involved step to take. But, one that maybe necessary if you truly have a "lemon".

After trying to resolve the issue with your RV dealer and manufacturer, contact your state to find out how to report a lemon. One of the most important parts is to keep accurate records. You will have to document when your house on wheels was in for service and exactly how they repaired the unit each time.

There is a federal law, The Magnuson-Moss Warranty Act that protects products that cost more than $25. Well, an RV definitely costs more than that. This law seems geared for automobiles, but definitely worth a try, especially if your state does not have a lemon law.

Check all this out in your research before you buy your RV. You are spending a lot of money for this "house" whether you live in it full time or not. Simply look up RV lemon law online and you will get all kinds of information to start your inquiry.

Friends for A Reason, A Season and Life

One of the old sayings tells us some people come into our lives for a reason; they're there to help us or teach us or show us something. Others find us for a reason; a project, a certain time in our lives, or through business and professions. Others are friends for a lifetime, even if we've only met them.

As you pull out of your community on your way to your RVing adventure, you'll leave behind some friends and move toward finding new ones. Saying goodbye is not always easy.

We pulled our new motorhome into our driveway, opened it up and invited in our friends and neighbors to take a look and have very modest refreshments. That way we said goodbye to everyone, and had a lot of laughter and memories while we did it.

Full-timer in Iowa

You can stay in touch. The wonder of our times is that you don't really have to say goodbye to your family and friends. As you'll read in this book, your computer will become your best friend. You can install Skype, the program that lets you see people while you talk to them. Your cell phone will be in your pocket.

While in the old days we stood in line at the telephone bank in campgrounds, today we sit in our pajamas and go online.

Expect some reactions. There will be times when you just plain miss things, whether it's your house, your garden, your family or your friends. These feelings will pass. You can make a call, talk to someone who understands or get on your email or Facebook or Twitter and talk online. It is normal and natural, whenever we give up something, to experience a sense of loss; to wonder why we ever did this, to question our decisions. You can ride it out – perhaps literally.

Meet people. Every new person you meet can become part of your community. If you are in a campground for more than a few days, invite people to go out for lunch. Find out who plays cards or your favorite board game. Look up activities for your area. There is a lot to do, and as the sign and picture says in one of the RV factories in Indiana, "When was the last time you met new best friends in a motel?" A campground brings a natural hometown community to you. Take advantage of it.

Grief on the Road

It happens to everyone at some time: a crisis back home, an illness. There is a death in the family. This is a time when it's important to take care of you as well as your loved ones.

Our daughter's husband fell from a roof he was working on and died. We were 800 miles away, and as soon as we got the phone call we started making arrangements to get back. I got a flight to her the next day. A friend helped my husband drive the camper back. You just have to know that no matter what happens you can handle it. Full-timer from Michigan

The great advantage to having an RV is that you are mobile. You can get there. And if someone dies and you absolutely can't get to the funeral, the funeral can come to you via internet or Skype if the family requests it and the funeral home can provide it.

Ask for help. This is a time to call on family and friends and fellow RVers. If you need help making reservations, ask at your campground office. If you need help driving back or if one of you needs to fly, ask for help. People want to be supportive in times of crisis. Let them.

Expect a lot of feelings. One of the emotions RVers talk about when something bad happens back home or with a family member is feeling guilty. Actually, what we feel is regret. Guilt comes after we purposefully and with intent hurt another emotionally, physically or mentally. Regret comes when we wish we could have done something different or feel we didn't do all we could. If you could have known what was going to happen, perhaps you would have done something different. If you could have prevented a tragedy, you would have. Don't think because you're the senior in your family you have to control everything. Whether it's family or friends, your job is to be supportive and do only what you can.

Cry when you need to cry. Spend a lot of time on the phone. Remember that worrying doesn't help anything tomorrow, it just takes away the peace of today. You have your computer and a store is nearby where you can get a notebook and pens or an attractive journal. Keep a journal, record your feelings and in a few months you can see you're making progress. While we never get over grief, we can make use of it, write about it, learn from it. Bad things really do happen to everyone, as you well know, whether you're on the road or behind a white picket fence.

Know, also, that you and your partner are likely to grieve differently. There are excellent books on how to handle grief available from www.centering.org. Outstanding online information about grief and sorrow is also available. Tom Golden's Webhealing.com is a good place to start.

You'll take your grief with you down the road, so honor it. Treat yourself with respect and take care of you.

Trips

Where have we been since RVing full time? We have primarily been east of the Mississippi River. When we rented we went to Civil War Battlefields and the Outer Banks. My husband is a Civil War re-enactor so he loved this. I did too as I no longer had to sit with the park ranger to be in the air conditioning. I could go rest in the comfort of my own RV.

The beach--ah, it is great to be at the beach and walk out your door to the ocean. You can be in your own bed and hear the waves crashing on the sand. What a way to be lulled into sleep.

My father-in-law was still living when we bought our first RV. After Ken's school was out for the summer we headed for Dubuque, Iowa. We would spend time with him helping him out and then go exploring in Minnesota and/or Wisconsin.

North of Duluth, Minnesota, on Lake Superior's rugged coast is a gorgeous drive up to Grand Moray. This was a pleasant surprise for us as we were just exploring around the lake and found this beautiful area.

Bayfield, Washburn, Ashland and the Apostle Islands in Wisconsin is another nearby jewel. The Big Blue Tent is Chautauqua on the Lake. Musical shows are presented all summer. Karlyn Holman offers water color painting classes, plus there are lots of water activities. This is a lovely area and we spent two 4th of Julys here.

One of them was beautiful weather with a parade of the locals that could have been held in any small town USA. The next year it was so cold that we had the heat on in the RV as the fireworks went off. (Keep in mind we are Floridians). Thank goodness, the local RV park is operated by the city and right on Lake Superior, so we had a front row seat for the fireworks.

On one of our trips to help Pop we continued on around Lake Superior through the upper peninsula (UP) of Michigan and across the Mackinaw Bridge. (We had to overnight north of the bridge as the wind was too strong for RV's and semi trucks to cross when we arrived) Also, check out campgrounds just south of the bridge with a great view of the lake and take the boat to Mackinaw Island.

Wherever your travels take you, keep a journal. I can teach journaling and I do a visual journal of our travels. This is just a collection of mementos that I keep with written documentation of what and where we have been.

What campground did we stay while we were at the Wisconsin Dells, look it up in your journal. I date each entry including the campground and city where we are staying.

This is a good habit to get into for future reference and memory time. Document however you feel comfortable. Some people do not like to write and collect post cards of the places they have been. What a quick and easy way to do this. Your pictures are always perfect also.

Super Bowl 2007

We went to bed thinking that the Indianapolis Colts had lost the AFC Championship game at the last minute. Our trip to Miami was off. Oh dear, what fun that would have been.

Around 2 AM, I hear screaming from the front of the coach. Ken couldn't sleep and had gotten up to learn the Colts had won. It was a sporting miracle for us. Fortunately, the campground had been closed, so I had not had the opportunity to cancel the reservations.

We left on Wednesday to drive down to Miami for the Super Bowl to played on Feb. 2, 2007. We were so excited as Indianapolis had never been to the Super Bowl before. What a week awaited us.

The NFL Experience is similar to a state fair geared for football and the 2 teams in the Super Bowl, the Indianapolis Colts and the Chicago Bears. There are a lot of physical activities, passing, punting, kicking, and anything you can do to a football. All kinds of games of physical chance.

The Super Bowl sponsors all have booths or activities. Macy's was a sponsor that year and we got to be "balloon handlers". It was just like being at the Macy's Thanksgiving Day Parade as we carried the football balloon down the street.

We got to send messages to the players, give advice to the coach, and get our pictures taken with the players (actually a blue screen). All part of the fun.

You get to see the Lombardi trophy up close, probably the only time you will ever get to do this. Boy, is security tight around that thing.

It was a fun filled day of activities. It is especially fun when it is your team in all the activities. We had been to the NFL Experience in Jacksonville, but to have it be your team is wonderful. Of course, we all bought Super Bowl clothes while we were there.

The next day we went to South Beach to watch the CBS Morning Show whose network was televising the game. We were arriving just as the night life was closing down. The show had Bobby Flay and John Legend as guests, plus the cheerleaders and mascots from each team. In addition to the show, there was barbecuing on the beach. What a way to start a day with a sunrise on the beach watching a live television show.

Afterwards we walked around as ESPN, CBS Sports and all the TV shows were gearing up for their daily sporting event shows. Occasionally, you caught a glimpse or could hear one of the players on one of the shows.

We had a late breakfast at one of the side walk cafes with all the other fans milling about. People selling tickets and some trying to buy tickets. We still did not have tickets for the game.

There are just all kinds of activities going on. Parties, parties, and more parties. Unless you are an invited guest like Paris Hilton, a Kardashian, or Tom Cruise these parties are very expensive. Hundreds to thousands of dollars for entry into each party. Always check the local TV and radio stations web sites, Facebook, or Twitters for complimentary tickets to some events and a list of activities.

We had been looking for tickets for Sunday's game without any luck. We checked all the web sites, Stubhub, Ticket Master, etc. and they were all running $3-5000 a ticket. That is way over our budget.

Sunday, the day of rain. It had been absolutely beautiful all week, we call it Chamber of Commerce weather as it had been sunny and beautiful. No sun today, just rain. It is the first time the Super Bowl game has been played in the rain.

No luck with tickets so far either. We go to the Seminole Hard Rock Hotel & Casino as there is a pre-Super Bowl party. They are drawing for game tickets. Some lucky people did get free tickets, but we did not.

Due to security there is no tailgating area near the stadium. Bummer, as that is where we were told was the best chance to get tickets at the last minute. No chance here.

We drove around the stadium in the rain. We could hear the National Anthem, see the flyover by the Air Force, and feel the rain, but no

tickets. We did have an opportunity to buy tickets for

$3000 after the game had started, but Ken passed on them just as a cheer went up. We didn't know it then, but Chicago had just scored the opening touchdown.

We drove back to the Seminole Hard Rock Hotel & Casino to watch the game at their sports bar. It was fun and dry, but it would have been more fun and much wetter at the stadium.

We were already there for the post-game party and what a celebration it was. Cheering, yelling, drinking by all of us in our blue and white clothes for the Colts.

National Political Convention

One of our most exciting trips was to volunteer at a National Political Convention. I started checking almost a year in advance for volunteer registration online and signed up with both parties. We answered every question and filled out all the forms. We heard back from both parties. The Democrats were filled and the Republicans still needed volunteers. We were headed to Minneapolis and the Republican National Convention.

Now this was not a small feat. This was the summer of $4+ a gallon for diesel. We almost backed out at the expense of the trip as we were in North Carolina at the time. But, we figured it was a once in a lifetime opportunity. We decided to go, but the fuel was costly.

We were assigned the Civic Fest prior to the convention which was great as we had our volunteer work done before the actual convention started. The Civic Fest was like a state fair based on our country's history. This is my husband's passion and vocation. He worked the political pins and memorabilia area and I  worked the welcome desk. We had a lot of fun and got to meet so many people.

I was right there at the welcome desk for the opening ceremony with the governor of Minnesota and their senator. Both would play interesting roles in our future as Gov. Tim Pawlenty was a finalist for the vice presidency at this convention and Senator Norm Coleman was involved in one of the closest races with now Senator Al Franken. By working this fest we also found out about other volunteer opportunities and worked a press event at Mill City Museum overlooking the Mississippi River.

To be part of this atmosphere is electrifying. At one point we were sitting at the CNN restaurant (they literally converted a local restaurant into their own place for the convention) having lunch with Wolf Blitzer and Candy Crowley as the speakers. To our left was Florida's then Senator Mel Martinez being interviewed live on CNN. To our right was Howard Dean live on the radio and in the corner were young people chatting live on the internet from the convention.

After the lunch, the CNN people took us to their

news booth in the convention hall. We were allowed to go down on the floor and take pictures. Our Christmas picture for 2008 was us with the Florida state sign on the convention floor. These are things that you normally only see on TV.

Most exciting of all was being able to get into the convention hall. We were there for the Roll Call of States to nominate a presidential candidate. I looked over at Ken and he was teary-eyed and said, "I have taught this for 35 years and to be able to see it actually happen in person is unbelievable."

We were there the first time Sarah Palin walked onto a national public stage. (You can imagine the rumors flying around the Civic Fest when her name was announced). We heard Senator John McCain make his acceptance speech for the nomination to be the Presidential candidate for this party. It would have been equally exciting if we had been at the Democratic convention. It wasn't the party. It was being part of history.

It was a celebration and lots of hoopla to get their people to go back home and work to get these candidates elected. The Democrats had done the same thing in Denver just a few weeks ago. You all know how the election turned out and where these people are today.

Ken inside the convention hall. He is oh, so happy as this has been a dream of his to attend a National Political Convention.

Washington DC

I cannot finish this book without telling about our ultimate volunteering experience. In 2009, we got to help decorate the White House. What a thrill that was!

While I was home recuperating in the mid 90's, HGTV ran a Christmas special showing volunteers decorating the White House. I thought, we can do this as we are crafty people.

I called my Congressman and they gave me a phone number to call. "White House", the operator said, as I dropped the phone. I started the process and it took me 12 years to get selected. I am persistent, if nothing else.

Once I got on the list for the White House Flower Shop in 2009, they were so helpful. I would call to see if they needed any more information or when I could I send emails or letters. Bob, who has since retired, was so patient and kept saying each administration does it differently and they weren't sure what President and Mrs. Obama had planned. Once the decisions were made, we started receiving all kinds of invitations and security clearance forms.

We were selected and going to DC! Now, we had to make plans to get there. Do we take the RV? There are no RV parks near downtown DC. Cherry Hill in College Park, Maryland is the closest one to a Metro station, but that is not convenient for a daily trip to the White House. Fairfax County Park in Vienna, Virginia is not open in the winter. We opted not to take the RV.

We decided on the train. We have an overnight train from Orlando to DC. We boarded on Thanksgiving Day at 1 PM. We upgraded to a roomette so that we would have a separate area to read and sleep. We thought this best for my breathing problems and it worked out very well. By upgrading, we also got our meals included in the trip.

We got into town in time to help out at the White House warehouse. Now, I would tell you where this is located, but we are sworn to secrecy. It is like a Home Depot or Lowe's except the shelves are loaded with things from past Presidents that they are storing.

We worked here for two days putting together the ribbons, floral pics, and sprigs of every known flower that you could imagine. It was a florists delight to be working with these splendid supplies. It was so interesting to meet and hear how the other volunteers had gotten selected as there was some from each state.

On day 3 we went to the White House. The anticipation was palatable as we all stood outside in the cold waiting for clearance to go inside to decorate the White House. Finally, we had all cleared and we followed our team leader (each member of the Flower Shop led a group of volunteers) to our assigned spot. Ken and I were on different teams and I went to the East Portico. We hung boughs of evergreens around those huge windows and put a big wreath in the center of each one. Another lady and I made bows for the wreaths and arches.

Oh my, I am actually here looking out of the White House windows past the Rose Garden to the Washington Monument. Every so often a man dressed in black with a machine gun came through the garden on his route to guard our President. Bo, the First Family's dog, also came through on his way outside. Now, we had been told not to call Bo over, but he came right over and we got to pet him. What a cutie.

There were 2 days decorating at the White House, plus eating breakfast in the Family Dining Room as the Obama's chose to eat upstairs. We had lunch and dinner in the State Dining Room with paper and plastic, but we were in the State Dining Room eating. Dinner at the White House had been on my "bucket list" and Ken had just laughed at me, asking how I was going to accomplish this? I had no idea, but here I was, twice blessed as I was there for 2 days.

The final night was a reception held by Mrs. Obama for the holiday and White House volunteers. We got to bring our cameras and take pictures of "our" decorations. What pride we had as we showed our new friends what we had decorated. The east entry way for guests, the Portico, the flowers we had worked with during our time there. Ken took us to the Blue Room for the Official Christmas Tree as he had helped decorate the top of it while on scaffolding. It was beautiful!

A military Jazz band played as we mingled at the party and the food was delicious and presented so gorgeously. Santa was there and Mrs. Obama made an appearance thanking us all for our work in making the White House decorated for the holidays. We all could have floated home from the party as our feet were definitely not touching the ground.

Ken was born and grew up in DC. His Dad worked for the US Government and Ken has wonderful memories of Easter Egg Hunts on the

White House lawn as a child. This was a whole different rewarding and once in a lifetime experience. It is a testament that dreams do come true for me.

This is a picture of Ken and me in front of "his" tree in the Blue Room.

Fun Photos on the Road

An Indianapolis Colts fan

Dog lovers,
especially Pugs

Clemson University fans

These are pictures taken on the road and I have no way of finding out the owners to give them credit. If you recognize your RV, contact me and I will acknowledge you in the next book.

Closing

Most books stop at *The End*, but ours is just starting. It is actually the beginning of a new life for us and you. Life on the open road, going where you want and when you want, visiting friends, relatives, and Grandchildren. What more could you ask for?

You must maintain your health. The average full time RVer gains 10 pounds on the road the first year. Well, I am above average! I didn't want to continue on this path. As a Registered Yoga Teacher (RYT), I also knew better. Our next book will show you how to remain healthy and flexible while living in an RV. It can work as we are living proof.

While on the road we can be contacted at any of the following.

www.ourhomeontheroad.com

ourhomeontheroad@gmail.com

www.facebook.com/ourhomeontheroad

www.twitter.com/@rhomeontheroad

Ken is a quilt appraiser and we make many quilt shows and museums throughout the US. We are currently presenting, "The Story of the Quilt during the Civil War", for the 150th anniversary. If you would like us to make a presentation to your quilt guild or historical association, please contact us at kgquiltappraiser@gmail.com. Check out his web site at www.Kenthequiltguy.com He does quilt appraisals and presentations on "The Care and Feeding of Quilts" and "Why do you Need a Quilt Appraisal".

We love being on the road and have no plans to stop at this time. We keep ourselves busy and healthy, so that we may have many more years on the road. Safe Driving to You All!

Recreational Vehicle Resources

Camping World   www.campingworld.com
    Bowling Green, Ky   888-626-7576

Escapees RV Club   www.escapees.com
    Livingston, Texas   888-757-2582

Family Motor Coach Association www.fmca.com
    Cincinnati, Ohio   800-543-3622

Good Sam's Club   www.goodsamclub.com
    Englewood, Colorado   800-234-3450

Lazydays RV Terms

120 AC *112* DC *I* LP-gas - The power sources on which RV refrigerators operate; 120 AC is 120-volt alternating current (same as in houses); 12 DC is 12-volt direct current (same as in motor vehicles); LPgas. Some RV refrigerators can operate on two of the three sources, others on all three.

ANODE ROD - an anode rod, when used in a water heater, attracts corrosion causing products in the water. These products attack the anode rod instead of the metal tank itself. The anode rod should be inspected yearly and changed when it is reduced to about 114of its original size. The rods are used in steel water heater tanks - an aluminum tank has an inner layer of anode metal to accomplish the same thing. Anode rods should not be installed in an aluminum tank!

AXLE RATIO - The ratio between the pinion and ring gears in the differential that multiply the torque provided by the engine. It is the number of drive line revolutions required to tum the axle one time. As an example, with a 4.10: 1 axle the drive line turns 4.1 times for each full axle revolution. The higher the number, the more torque and thus more towing power. However, the higher the number also means less speed.

BLACK WATER - disposal water from toilet system, held in holding tank until you dump it, in large tanks or dumping station available at most campgrounds. See: http://www.rverscorner.comlarticles/tanks.html

BRAKE ACTUATOR - a device mounted under the dash of a towing vehicle to control the braking

system of the trailer. Most Brake Actuators a based on a time delay, the more time the tow vehicle brakes

are applied the "harder" the trailer brakes are applied.

BRAKE CONTROLLER - a device mounted under the dash of a towing vehicle to control the braking system of the trailer. The Brake Controller senses the amount of braking force of the tow vehicle and applied a proportional force to the trailer braking system.

BTU - British Thermal Unit - A measurement of heat that is the quantity required to raise the temperature of one pound of water 1 degree F. RV air-conditioners and furnaces are BTU-rated.

CAMBER - Wheel alignment - Camber is the number of degrees each wheel is off of vertical. Looking from the front, tops of wheels farther apart than bottoms means "positive camber". As the load pushes the front end down, or the springs get weak, camber would go from positive to none to negative (bottoms of wheels farther apart than tops).

CASTOR - Wheel alignment - The steering wheels' desire to return to center after you turn a corner.

CONDENSATION - condensation is a result of warn moisture laden air contacting the cold window glass. Keeping a roof vent open helps to reduce the humidity levels. Those added roof vent covers help to prevent cold air from dropping down through the vent while still allowing moist air to escape. Using the roof vent fan when showering or the stove vent fan when cooking also helps prevent excess moisture buildup.

CONVERTER - A converter is device that converts 120 volt A/C (alternating current) to 12 volt DC (direct current). The RV devices mostly run on 12 volt DC power that is supplied by the battery, which allows the RV to function independently. When "shore power" (an electrical supply) is available, the converter changes the voltage from 120 to 12 volt to supply the appliances and to recharge the battery.

DINETTE - booth-like dining area. Table usually drops to convert unit into a bed at night.

DSI IGNITION - direct spark ignition - this term refers to the method of igniting the main burner on a propane fired appliance. The burner is lit with an electric spark and the flame is monitored by an electronic circuit board. This ignition system is used in refrigerators, furnaces and water heaters. There is now a version of stove tops that light the burners with a DSI ignition.

DUCTED AC is air conditioning supplied through a ducting system in the ceiling. This supplies cooling air at various vents located throughout the RV.

DUCTED HEAT is warm air from the furnace supplied to various locations in the RV through a ducting system located in the floor. (Similar to house heating systems)

DUAL ELECTRICAL SYSTEM - RV equipped with lights, appliances which operate on 12-volt battery power when self-contained, and with a converter, on 110 AC current when in campgrounds or with an onboard generator.

DUALLY - A pickup truck, or light-duty tow vehicle, with four tires on one rear axle.

GENERATOR - An engine powered device fuelled by gasoline or diesel fuel, and sometimes propane, for generating 120-volt AC power.

GREY WATER - disposal water from sinks, shower. In some units, this is held in a tank separate from black water; is also dumped in tanks at campgrounds.

GROSS AXLE WEIGHT RATING (GAWR) - The manufacturer's maximum load weight, in pounds, that can be placed on the axle. If an axle has a 3500-lb. GAWR and the RV has two axles (tandem axles), then the RV would have a Gross Vehicle Weight Rating (GVWR) of 7000 lbs.

GROSS COMBINED WEIGHT RATING (GCWR) - The manufacturers maximum load weight, in pounds, allowed for the trailer and tow vehicle. This rating includes the weight of the trailer and tow vehicle plus fuel, water, propane, supplies and passengers.

GROSS VEHICLE WEIGHT RATING (GVWR) - The manufacturers maximum load weight, in pounds, allowed for the vehicle. This rating includes the weight of the vehicle plus fuel, water, propane, supplies and passengers.

GROSS TRAILER WEIGHT (GTW) - Gross trailer weight is the weight of the trailer fully loaded in its actual towing condition. GTW is measured by placing the fully loaded trailer on a vehicle scale. The entire weight of the trailer should be supported on the scale.

HEAT EXCHANGER - A heat exchanger is a device that transfers heat from one source to another. For example, there is a heat exchanger in your furnace - the propane flame and combustion products are contained inside the heat exchanger that is sealed from the inside area. Inside air is blown over the surface of the exchanger, where it is warmed and the blown through the ducting system for room heating. The combustion gases are vented to the outside air.

HEAT STRIP - A heat strip is an electric heating element located in the air conditioning system with the warm air distributed by the air conditioner fan and ducting system. They are typically 1500 watt elements (about the same wattage as an electric hair dryer) and have limited function. Basically they "take the chill off'

HITCH WEIGHT - The amount of a trailer's weight that rests on the tow vehicle's hitch. For travel trailers this weight should be 10% to 15% of the total weight of the trailer. For fifth wheels this weight should be 15% to 20% of the total weight of the trailer.

HOLDING TANKS - There are three different holding tanks on most RVs; fresh water tank, gray water tank and black water tank. The fresh water tank holds fresh water that can be stored for later use. The gray water tank holds the waste water from the sinks and showers. The black water tank holds the waste from the toilet. See: http://www.rverscorner.comlarticles/tanks.html

HOOKUPS - The ability of connecting to a campground's facilities. The major types of hookups are electrical, water and sewer. If all three of these hookups are available, it is termed full hookup. Hookups may also include telephone and cable TV in some campgrounds.

INVERTER - An inverter is a device that changes 12 volt battery power to 120 volt AC power. It is used when "boon docking" (camping without hookups) to power certain 120 VAC only devices like a microwave oven. The amount of available power depends on the storage capacity of the batteries and the wattage rating of the inverter.

LAMINATE - A sandwich of structural frame members, wall paneling, insulation and exterior covering, adhesive-bonded under pressure and/or heat to form the RV's walls, floor and/or roof.

LIVABILITY PACKAGES - items to equip a motor home for daily living, which may be rented at nominal cost from rental firm, rather than brought from home. Include bed linens, pillows and blankets, bath towels, pots and pans, kitchen utensils, cutlery.

LP GAS - Liquefied Petroleum Gas. LP gas is used to fuel appliances in the RV, such as the stove, oven, water heater and refrigerator. Propane tanks are usually rated as pounds or gallons.

NET CARRYING CAPACITY (NCC) or Payload Capacity - Sometimes called the payload capacity, this is the maximum weight of fuel, water, propane, supplies and passengers that can be added to an RV without exceeding the Gross Vehicle Weight Rating (GVWR).

PILOT - a pilot is a small standby flame that is used to light the main burner of a propane fired appliance when the thermostat calls for heat. Pilots can be used in furnaces, water heaters, refrigerators, ovens and stove tops.

LIQUID PROPANE - LPG, or liquefied petroleum gas, used in RVs for heating, cooking and refrigeration. Also called bottle gas, for manner in which it is sold and stored.

RIG - what many RVer's call their units.

ROOF AIR CONDITIONING - air conditioning unit mounted on roof ofRV, to cool the RV when it is parked. When moving, most RVs are cooled by separate air conditioning units which are components of the engine, or they may be cooled by a roof top if a proper size generator is installed.

RV - short for Recreation Vehicle, a generic term for all pleasure vehicles which contain living accommodations. Multiple units are RVs and persons using them are RVer's.

SELF CONTAINED - RV which needs no external electrical, drain or water hookup. Thus, it can park overnight anywhere. Of course, self-contained units can also hook up to facilities when at campgrounds.

THERMOCOUPLE - a thermocouple is a device that monitors the pilot flame of a pilot model propane appliance. If the pilot flame is extinguished the thermocouple causes the gas valve to shut off the flow of gas to both the pilot flame and the main burner.

TOAD - A "toad" is an RV'ers term referring to a vehicle that is towed behind a motor home. Some vehicles can be towed without any modifications - others cannot be towed at all or at least without extensive alterations. For more information on this subject: http://www.towingworld.comlvehicle.html

TOE - Wheel alignment - Toe is the measure of whether the front of the wheels (looking down from the top) are closer (toe-in) or farther (toe-out) than the back of the wheels.

TONGUE WEIGHT - Tongue weight (TW) is the downward force exerted on the hitch ball by the trailer coupler. In most cases, it is about 10 to 15 percent ofGTW. TW of up to 300 lbs. can be measured on a household scale by resting the trailer coupler on the scale and placing the scale on a box so that the coupler is at its normal towing height. The trailer must be fully loaded and level. For heavier tongue weights, place a household scale and a brick that's as thick as the scale three feet apart. Set a length of pipe on each and rest a beam across the pipes. Re-zero the scale to correct for the weight of the beam and pipe. Securely block the trailer wheels. Rest the trailer jack on the beam, one (1) foot from the pipe on the brick and two (2) feet from the pipe on the scale. To obtain the TW, multiply the scale reading by three (3). For greater tongue weights, place the scale and brick four (4) feet apart, rest the jack on the beam three (3) feet from the scale and multiply the scale reading by four (4).

UNDERBELLY - The RV's under floor surface, which is protected by a weatherproofed material.

UNLOADED VEHICLE WEIGHT (UVW) or Dry Weight - Sometimes called the Dry Weight; it is the weight of the RV without adding fuel, water, propane, supplies and passengers. The manufacturers unloaded vehicle weight (UVW) will not include any dealer-installed options.

WASTE WATER TANKS - The gray water tank holds the waste water from the sinks and showers. The black water

tank holds the waste from the toilet. See: http://
www.rverscorner.comlarticles/tanks.htrnl

WET WEIGHT - The weight of the vehicle with the fuel,
freshwater and propane tanks full.

WHEELBASE - Distance between center lines of the
primary axles of a vehicle. If a motor home includes a tag
axle, the distance is measured from the front axle to the
center point between the drive and tag axles.

Terms, Motorized RV's, and Towable RV's (page 13-14) were provided
by Lazydays RV, Inc., Seffner, FL 33584
888-500-5299

Ken was a National Board Certified US History and government teacher for 35 years in the public school system. He taught 20 years at the middle school level in Indiana, 15 years at the high school level in Florida, and was an Adjunct Professor at Valencia Community College.

During that time he was a head swim and currently works seasonally at Walt Disney World. He is involved in Civil War re-enacting, which is his favorite time in US History. As a re-enactor, he needed a quilt to keep him warm at night. Connie helped him make the first quilt and now he makes and sells them to other re-enactors.

Ken got involved with the study of the history of quilts and has become a Professional Quilt Appraiser, working all over the United States as we travel. We are currently presenting "The Story of the Quilt During the Civil War" to quilt guilds and historical societies throughout the United States.

He is a sports enthusiast following Purdue University, his Alma Mater, the Indianapolis Colts, and Washington Redskins. He is on the Dean's Advisory Council of the College of Education at Purdue University, visiting the campus at least twice a year. He also plays in the Alumni Band, is an avid golfer, and volunteers as a "standard bearer" for the PGA Disney Golf Classic and the Arnold Palmer Invitational.

Connie Gleason, Masters Degree in Adult Education from Indiana University, Registered Yoga Teacher (RYT), Laughter Leader and clown. She has worked in the travel industry all her adult life as an airline employee, travel agent, tour escort, and was an adjunct professor in the Hospitality Management School at the University of Central Florida.

Connie grew up in Kokomo, Indiana and lived for 20 years in Indianapolis before transferring to Orlando with the airlines. Connie and Ken took full advantage of the flying benefits visiting the Orient, Mexico, Hawaii, and Europe several times. Once she became ill, she was grounded.

How she overcame the obstacles of living as a chemically sensitive person with breathing problems led to RVing and ultimately life on the road.

Giving back is a high priority for Connie and she volunteers at many events wherever she travels as her health allows. She is a member of Retired Senior Volunteer Program (RSVP) in Orlando. She volunteers in summers with the Swannanoa Gathering, Montreat, and the Roads Scholars programs in North Carolina and Florida.

CPSIA information can be obtained at www.ICGtesting.com
Printed in the USA
LVOW111005190312

273734LV00001B/1/P